Hanna-Barbera's

THE GREATEST ADVENTURE

STORIES FROM THE BIBLE

MOSES

text by
Christine L. Benagh

Based on a script by Harvey Bullock

ABINGDON PRESS
Nashville

Two young friends, Derek and Margo, are taking part in a very important dig in the Middle East. It is the opportunity of a lifetime for them to accompany her father, an archaeologist, on this expedition.

Most days their young nomad friend Moki, who is very curious about these things, joins them to ask a hundred questions and to keep things generally lively.

One especially hot and tiring day, the three friends are digging in their assigned spot, when the sand suddenly begins to give way. "Quick sand," shouts Moki as the three

MOSES

Copyright © 1986 by Hanna-Barbera Productions, Inc.

ISBN 0-687-15740-4

MANUFACTURED BY THE PARTHENON PRESS AT NASHVILLE, TENNESSEE, UNITED STATES OF AMERICA

spiral down, down, down in a funnel of
sand.

Then just as unexpectedly the air is clear,
and they are in an enormous room. What a
spectacle! It is filled with treasure of every
sort—vases, jars, statues, jewelry and
ornaments, pillars, furniture of gold and
ivory.

"How magnificent," whispers Derek in
awe.

"Wow," murmurs Moki.

Margo has moved ahead of the others
toward a huge bronze door. The latch
fastening the two massive panels is a
golden scarab beetle. She puts her hand on
the scarab, translating its message: *All who
enter here go back in time.* Suddenly, the
great doors swing open into what appears
to be a cavern of light.

"Come on," she calls, and without
hesitation the others follow.

They step over the threshold and —

Sudden and sharp as a lightning flash, the storm burst upon the three friends, snatching them off their feet, blinding and choking them with swirling sand.

Margo clutched Derek's shirt as she struggled to her feet, and the little group inched forward.

"A sand blizzard!" shouted Moki, working hard to keep his hat on his head and his feet underneath him.

"Where did it come from?" choked Margo, slipping and sliding as she tried to move ahead. "I feel as if I have been blown and tumbled for a thousand miles."

Derek turned and yelled over the roar, "I think I can make out a wall. Come on."

They huddled against the great stones of the wall gasping for breath. Then, as suddenly as it had started, the storm stopped.

"Do you have any idea where we are?" asked Derek, shaking the sand out of his clothes.

"At the beach." Moki brushed the sand from his hair and was about to empty his shoes when Margo called. The boys rushed to where she was standing some distance behind the wall.

"This has to be Egypt," gasped Derek.

"Or a museum," ventured Moki.

Margo ignored him. "It all looks so new and fresh. Why its ancient Egypt before it was ancient! We're looking at the Sphinx and the Pyramids when they were new."

"Wonder if we can discover how they were made?" said Derek. "That is one of the great mysteries of the world, you know."

Just then, a voice boomed behind them. "Quick, get those slaves over here."

A huge man advanced on the trio, holding an ugly whip in his hand. The look on his face said he didn't mind using it.

"A real Egyptian," whispered Margo.

"You were expecting an Eskimo?" Moki muttered from the corner of his mouth.

"Did you say slaves?" Derek gasped.

"So—you thought you would escape in the storm," growled the slavemaster. "Back to the brickyard, all of you." He cracked his whip, and they did not feel they could argue.

"I think we're going to learn how to make pyramids the hard way," said Moki.

What had promised to be an exciting adventure turned out to be hard, backbreaking labor. Derek, Moki, and Margo spent the day carrying the largest

bricks they had ever seen and loading them on the scaffolding for a construction project. Other slaves were making the bricks, mixing clay and straw, shaping the bricks and setting them to dry in the scorching sun. Not a moment's rest was permitted. The slavemaster saw to that.

"I can't wait for the sun to go down," sighed Margo.

"Where will we sleep?" wondered Derek.

"It won't matter," said Moki, "I'm so tired I can sleep standing up if that big brute will look the other way."

At last the day did come to an end. The slavemaster barked the order, snapped his whip, and the slaves hobbled away to their huts. The three friends began to look around. There might be some way to escape.

An old slave approached. "You are newcomers? Come, I will give you shelter."

"How kind, thank you," said Margo. "Uh . . . may I ask you something? We are sort of confused. We have some idea of where we are, but we are not sure *when* we are."

The old man stared at her.

"Well, can you just tell us what is going on?" asked Derek. "Who are you? Why are you a slave?"

"I am Elihu, a Hebrew, and my people have lived in Egypt for more than four hundred years. At first we were the king's friends, our teachers tell us, but then the pharaohs grew afraid because there were so many of us, and we were so healthy and strong. The pharaohs have done many cruel things to make our life hard. Since the great building projects started, my people have been forced to labor making bricks. Bricks, bricks, millions of them, to put into these never-ending buildings that reach to the sky."

"You are an Israelite!" exclaimed Derek, "and a slave in Egypt. That means this is about . . . ah . . ."

"It means this is about 1200 B.C.," put in Margo excitedly.

Elihu continued to stare, but then his eyes widened and he was looking beyond them at something.

"Can it be?" the old man stammered. "It must be. Even after all these years, I would recognize him, and that must be Aaron with him." He began to run toward the two figures approaching. "Moses, Moses, you have returned."

"Golly, Moses!" exclaimed Moki.

The two men came on steadily toward the cluster of slave huts. Elihu kept shouting and hopping about, and people began to appear in their doorways and gather round Moses and Aaron.

Moses raised his hand in greeting, and the people stood in silence. "I have come," he began, "because the Lord, the God of our fathers, has sent me. I bring his message to Pharaoh. God commands that Pharaoh set our people free. We are to leave Egypt, and I will lead you by God's command back to the land of Abraham. It is a rich land, flowing with good things, with milk and with honey."

There was a cheer from the crowd.

"I go now to Pharaoh to tell him he must let our people go. You, you must prepare yourselves to leave Egypt and to make a long journey."

There was another roar from the people, and they began to chatter with one another. Moses and Aaron moved away into the darkness toward the palace.

"Oh, Elihu," said Margo, "this is too exciting to miss. Please, show us the way to the palace."

Elihu hesitated, "I am tired, but there will be no sleep this night . . ."

"Of course not," added Moki. "Just think, you will be free; you won't have to do all this hard work. You don't look happy, Elihu."

"I cannot be," said Elihu. "I do not think Pharaoh will give up his laborers so easily."

"But Moses has said . . ." Derek began.

Elihu interrupted, "And what will Pharaoh say? Come, I know one of the guards who is not a bad fellow. We *will* watch this meeting."

The four hid behind the great column and watched Pharaoh. He was leaning from his golden chair questioning Moses. "How is it you dare to come into my presence when you were not summoned?"

"I am here, O Pharaoh, because my God commands it. I was a tender of sheep in the desert, and one day at the foot of a great and holy mountain I saw a bush burning. I was engulfed in flames, and yet the leaves and branches were not harmed.

As I looked at this wonder, a voice from the bush called me by name. 'I am the God of your fathers and of your people. I have seen their misery. Go to Pharaoh and tell him to let my people go.' "

Aaron stepped forward, "And so, great Pharaoh, we ask you to free the people as our God commands, so that we may go away from Egypt and worship our God as we should."

Pharaoh roared, "What god can command Pharaoh?"

"He is the God of all," said Moses. "He is angry because you hold his people in slavery. I beg you to listen to his commands so that your land may escape his punishments."

At this Pharaoh threw back his head and laughed. "Can the god of slaves have power of the ruler of Egypt?"

At this Aaron turned and hurled his rod to the floor. Immediately it became a writhing cobra. It slithered to within a foot of where the watchers were hiding and coiled there menacingly.

It took only a moment for Pharaoh to recover his poise. "It is but a trick of the eye. My own magicians can do as much." He clapped his hands and they came forward.

They too had rods in their hands. They raised them, muttering some strange words, and threw them to the floor. Their rods too became snakes, a little smaller than Aaron's.

"You see," said Pharaoh, "your God has no great power. It was from Egyptian sorcerers that he learned the trick."

"I beg you, royal Pharaoh, do not mock the great God of all. Egypt will surely suffer." Moses was very solemn.

"Observe, O Pharaoh," whispered the head magician, "our serpents are being consumed by that other one."

"That means nothing," said Pharaoh. "Egypt will suffer only if we lose our laborers. Our great buildings, our magnificence depend on them. Be gone."

Moses and Aaron slowly left the throne room.

Elihu waited outside with Margo, Derek, and Moki. "Moses, old friend," he said, "do not go on with this madness. Pharaoh will never let us go free, and I see only trouble ahead."

"I must obey the Lord," said Moses with bowed head. "Have patience, you will be free. We will go to Pharaoh again tomorrow when he is at the river palace."

Before daybreak Moki, Margo, and Derek were at the river's edge. They quietly untied a small boat and rowed toward the palace silhouetted against the sunrise.

Pharaoh's pavillion on the river was as grand as his palace in the city. Wide stone steps led down into the waters of the Nile, and handsome walls set off the part in which Pharaoh was bathing as the chief of his magicians approached. "The two Hebrew sorcerers are here, O Pharaoh, and desire to speak with you. Shall I send them away?"

"Let them come here. What can two wretched slaves do against the gods of Egypt and their Pharaoh?"

Moses descended the steps. "We have come, O Pharaoh, to say once more that the Lord, our God, demands that you release the people of Israel."

Aaron held his rod high and added, "We have a sign from our God. This great river whose waters are the life of the land of Egypt will become blood."

Even as he spoke the waters began to change. They became pinkish and then deep, thick blood red.

From their hideout in the reeds nearby, the three friends watched and could hardly believe their eyes. Margo lifted the hand she had been dangling in the water and gasped, "This is real blood!"

Pharaoh hurried out of the foul water and glared at the visitors as his servants dried him off and brought fresh robes.

"You will not frighten the divine Pharaoh with your tricks. My wisemen and magicians can do as much and more. I will call them into council. Meanwhile, your people will have some additional work."

Derek and the others were so sure that this sign would convince Pharaoh of God's power that they had hurried back to the slave settlement. Moki ran ahead calling out, "Moses has done it! Moses has done it! The river and all the waters of Egypt have been turned to blood. Pharaoh will have to let you go."

"What the lad says is true." Elihu was speaking from the village well. From the bucket in his hand poured bright red liquid.

But the slaves did not have long to rejoice. Hurrying wheels clanged, and a cloud of dust billowed up around the chariot of the Overseer of Slaves. "Fall into work parties at once," he shouted. "Before you make your daily quota of bricks you must dig wells in the city and around the palace—dig until you find good water." He stood in the chariot with his arms folded. The slavemasters herded the weary Hebrews out of the compound.

Moki climbed into the last cart with Elihu, and waved for his friends to get on. As they bumped and jolted toward the city they passed Moses and Aaron coming along the road. Elihu struggled to his feet and called out as they passed, "You are not freeing us, you Moses. We are worse off than before you came."

Moses raised his head, "Do not doubt, my friend," he said. "Our God is not finished; there is yet another sign."

"What else do you suppose could happen?" Margo wondered aloud. Even as she spoke a large green frog hopped into the cart. Moki caught the little creature and was showing it around, when another frog jumped on, and then another and another. Suddenly there were frogs everywhere.

They were indeed the Lord's plague. They covered the land of Egypt. They were thick in the finest houses. They invaded the council of the court magicians. They hopped and croaked in the royal kitchen and bed chamber, and no one could keep them out of the banquet hall.

At last a weary Pharaoh
sent for Moses.
"Pray to your God for us so
that he will take these
loathsome frogs out of the
land. When they are gone, I
will let the people go."

"They will be gone
tomorrow," promised Moses,
"and so we also will be
gone."

"Tomorrow," nodded
Pharaoh.

But the next day as the Hebrews were packing their belongings and loading their carts, the Overseer of Slaves pushed into their midst cracking his whip and dispatching his gang masters to get the people back to work.

Placing himself in front of the chariot, Moses addressed the officer. "There must be some mistake. Pharaoh has authorized this; we are preparing to leave Egypt with his permission."

"I act now under Pharaoh's order," snapped the man. "He has had a change of mind." Unload those carts and return to work, all of you. We are increasing your work. Then you will have no time to sit around plotting to escape."

Aaron had come to Moses' side. "Tell your master that our God will not be mocked. There are yet terrible punishments in store for Egypt if he will not let us go."

For many months terrible plagues did come upon the land, and the people suffered greatly. Not only Pharaoh and his courtiers, but the ordinary people, and even beggars in the street. The Hebrew slaves also suffered, not from the plagues, but because after each disaster Pharaoh would promise to let them go and then change his mind and make their work still harder. They received less and less food and more and more beatings, until they were very discouraged.

Moses gathered them together to reassure them, reminding them of God's great promises to deliver and help them.

"Is this what you call help?" cried Elihu. His voice was shrill, and he was shaking with anger. "You are the plague against us, Moses. The voices you hear at night, they cannot be from God, for his signs only add to our suffering."

"Take care, Elihu," said Moses. "You are tempting the Lord God, who has sent these signs and wonders to show his might to Pharaoh."

Elihu was beside himself, "What good have the plagues done? None. Think back, after the frogs came the swarms of lice and flies that filled the air until one could not see his hand before his face nor take a breath of air. Oh, Pharaoh promised to let us go once you had rid the land of flies, but did he? No. Did he ease our burden of work? No.

"Then there was the plague upon the cattle. Their animals dropped in the fields until none was left. Dead beasts lay everywhere. You halted the plague when Pharaoh promised to release us, but did he keep his word? No. Did our life get easier? No.

"The boils that tormented the Egyptians were terrible, but the plague of storms was even more dreadful. Who had ever before seen such lightning running like fire along the ground or heard such deafening thunder? And the hailstones, so huge they tore the trees and plants to bits. Oh, Pharaoh was frightened, it is true, and said we could leave Egypt. But did he permit it? No. Did he lighten the work of the people who have such a god? No.

"Then came the locusts, clouds and clouds of them, and they ate every leaf and blade of grass that had not been ruined by the hail. Are we free because of that? No."

"God have mercy on you, Elihu," said Moses. "It is not Pharaoh only who will not believe. It is God's own people."

"Listen to us," Aaron stepped forward. "The Lord's next sign is one that will be felt heavily by all of Egypt. You must have faith. We will be free."

The gathering was broken up by the slavemasters collecting Hebrews onto the carts to be hauled to work. As usual Elihu and his young friends were at the end of the procession.

"If I thought we had a chance, I would jump our driver, turn the cart off the road, and head for those reeds to try to escape," said Derek.

"We might have a chance if we got his whip first," said Margo.

"What have we got to lose?" asked Moki. "Are you with us, Elihu?" The old man nodded.

Derek crept forward with Elihu and Moki crouched beside him. Derek threw both arms around the driver's throat at the same moment that Elihu and Moki each grabbed an arm. Margo sprang for the whip and climbed into the driver's seat as the driver tumbled from the cart. She jerked the cart sharply to the right and tried to urge the horses.

They were not going fast enough, but at least they were going. Then, it was as if the light had been switched off. It was pitch dark.

"Where are the headlights?" squeaked Moki.

"At least no one can see us," said Derek as they climbed down from the cart and groped about.

"This is the plague," moaned Elihu. "It is a curtain of thick darkness. I can feel it on my skin."

The heavy black pall lay over Egypt for three days, and in the royal palace there was gloom and despair. "Go bring that Moses to me," said Pharaoh. "This darkness I cannot bear."

When Moses and Aaron appeared before Pharaoh, the ruler of Egypt seemed much changed.

"I see that your God is a great God," he said. "I have sinned against him, I will let you go, and I will not change my mind. I want you and all your people out of my land forever. Only your animals, your cattle and sheep, you must leave here in Egypt."

Aaron addressed the king, "You are asking the impossible. We worship our God with animal offerings, and we depend on them for food. Without the cattle, we will die on our journey."

"I have spoken," roared Pharaoh. "Leave your cattle, or you must stay in Egypt. One thing more, never enter my presence again. If I see you again, you shall die."

"You have spoken truly," said Moses quietly. "You shall never see my face again. The next plague will be brought by the Angel of Death."

Moses and Aaron called a solemn assembly of the slaves. "Hear me, O people

of Israel, the Lord our God will very soon visit Egypt, sending the Angel of Death at midnight to strike the firstborn in every home—the palace of Pharaoh and the poorest cottage."

"Does Pharaoh know this?" asked Elihu.

"We gave him warning this morning, but he scoffed at us. What more can we do?" answered Aaron.

"It will be a night of nights for us," continued Moses. "The Lord will make a difference between our people and the Egyptians. The Angel of Death will visit their houses, but our houses he will pass over if you do as he commands. Each family is to kill a lamb to be eaten on this night of the Lord's Passover. You are to dip a switch of herbs into the lamb's blood and mark your doorways, overhead and on either side. When the angel sees the blood, no harm will come to those in that house.

"On that night there will be no time for packing. Pharaoh will send us out without delay. So make ready now."

It happened just as Moses had said. The Angel of Death went throughout Egypt, and sorrow was in every house. Pharaoh rose from his bed and sent a messenger to Moses commanding him to take the people and all their belongings and to go out of the land, taking the curse of death with them.

And so after the long years of suffering and bondage the people were free. Their

carts were loaded with bundles and baskets and hampers. A joyous procession moved through the land of Egypt.

Moses encouraged the people, "You need have no fear of getting lost, for the Lord himself is leading us. See that pillar of bright cloud. It is the Lord's presence. Just follow and all will be well." The cloud led them to the edge of the wilderness not far from the sea, and there it stopped.

The people had hardly gone a full day's journey when Pharaoh began to be sorry he had let them go. "These people have been a great trouble and sorrow to us," he said. "Pharaoh shall be revenged upon these wretched slaves who think they can ruin Egypt. Call the captain of my chariots. We will get them back. We can overtake them easily; they are on foot and have much baggage."

All the army of the Egyptians, with six hundred swift chariots, galloped off in pursuit of the Hebrews. The lead charioteer gave a shout when he spotted their camp, and he sent a scout to take word to Pharaoh that the runaways were trapped between the army and the sea.

"We have them," cried Pharaoh. "Forward! Spread your chariots. Do not slow down."

The Hebrews saw the Egyptians approaching, and they were afraid. "Look what you have done," cried one old man to Moses. "You have brought us here to die. Why did you not leave us alone? At least in Egypt we would have graves. Here we will be driven into the sea."

"Be still," cried Moses, "you are going to see the strength of the Lord." But even as he spoke, Pharaoh and his horsemen came nearer and nearer.

"Now," shouted Moses above the wind that was rising steadily. He held out his rod over the waters of the sea, and before the astonished eyes of the three friends and all the people of Israel the waters of the sea divided into two great walls of water with a deep furrow going between.

"Move forward. Do not tarry. Go in at once."

The people obeyed him. Onto the seabed they marched, moving steadily until they came to the other side.

The army of Egypt was by this time at the edge of the water. Pharaoh saw the hated Hebrews going safely up on the other side. In a frenzy he urged his men forward, and they too plunged into the wide furrow.

They had not gone far before the horses

began to sink and stumble in the wet sand. The heavy chariots mired down, and the wheels began to break and come off. The great army had almost come to a standstill when, with a sudden roar and a rush, the waters closed over them.

Moses, who had all this time been holding up his rod, fell to his knees in grateful prayer, and all the people knelt and worshiped.

Next morning the procession formed again, and the bright cloud moved ahead.

Derek, Margo, and Moki were feeling very tired and a little sad. A solemn and important time was coming to an end for them. They moved along the column of people until they found their friend Elihu.

Derek spoke first. "We can't go with you into the wilderness, old friend. We would only getting farther and farther from where we belong."

"We'll never forget you," said Margo. "Or Moses," added Moki. "What a man!"

"I fear," said the old man sadly, "that when you think of these times, you will remember how weak my faith was and how often I doubted our God and our great leader. This was a test of the faith of all my people, and we did not pass that test with honor. But our God is good to us, and now we are truly on the way to our own promised land. May he be with you in yours. Farewell."